# THE ROMANCE OF FOOD

**THE ROMANCE OF FOOD**

Wherein a goodly number of authors
serve up their most agreeable thoughts
concerning a variety of tasty subjects
among which are

A Soup Song
A Snack! A Snack!
Queen Elizabeth I, Pays a Visit
Mushrooms for Breakfast
Pasta!
The Origins of Beer
Love and Cooking
The Bake Sale
Words From the Wise in Wine
&
The Elephant Cutlet

Edited by Frederick Heider and Barbara Loots

Hallmark Crown Editions

The publisher wishes to thank those who have given their kind permission to reprint material included in this book. Every effort has been made to give proper acknowledgments. Any omissions or errors are deeply regretted, and the publisher, upon notification, will be pleased to make necessary corrections in subsequent editions.

Acknowledgments: "Love and Cooking" from *Papa D: A Saga of Love and Cooking*, by Edward G. Danziger. ©1967 by John F. Blair, Publisher. Reprinted by permission. John 6:24-35; Joshua 5:6; Deuteronomy 8:3; Proverbs 15:17; Ecclesiastes 8:15; and Matthew 6:11 from the *King James Version Bible*. Reprinted by permission of the Cambridge University Press. Published by the Syndics of Cambridge University Press. "The Algonquin" by Gertrude Athearton and "More About the Algonquin" by O. O. McIntyre from *Tales of a Wayward Inn* by Frank Case. Copyright 1938 by Frank Case. Copyright renewed 1966. Reprinted by permission of Carroll Case. "A Grain of Genesis" from the *Holy Bible*. Copyright ©Confraternity of Christian Doctrine 1952. Used by permission of the copyright owner. "The Rite of Hospitality" from *Kitchen and Table* by Colin Clair. Copyright ©1964 by Colin Clair. Reprinted by permission of Abelard-Schuman, Publisher. "Thomas Jefferson Entertains" from *American Food: The Gastronomic Story* by Evan Jones. Copyright ©1974, 1975 by Evan Jones and Judith B. Jones. Reprinted by permission of the publisher, E. P. Dutton & Co., Inc. "Land of the Pilgrims' Pride" taken from *Hung, Strung and Potted* by Sally Smith Booth. ©1971 by Sally Smith Booth. Used by permission of Crown Publishers, Inc. "Up and Down" from *Below Stairs* by Margaret Powell. Copyright ©1968 by Margaret Powell and Leigh Crutchley. Reprinted by permission of Dodd, Mead & Company, Inc. and Peter Davies, Ltd. "Shape Up or Sing as a Group," copyright ©1970, 1971, 1972, 1973 by Field Enterprises, Inc.; copyright ©1970, 1971, 1972 by The Hearst Corporation, from *I Lost Everything in the Post-Natal Depression* by Erma Bombeck. Used by permission of Doubleday & Company, Inc. "A Feast of Nations" reprinted with the permission of Farrar, Straus & Giroux, Inc. from *Foods America Gave the World* by A. Hyatt Verrill, Copyright 1937 by L. C. Page & Company, Inc., copyright renewed 1965 by Leda Ruth Verrill. "Morocco" by Rupert Croft-Cooke reprinted by permission from the December 1968 issue of *Gourmet*. Excerpt ("In the Good Old Summertime") from pp. 96-97 in *Mark Twain's Autobiography*, Vol. I, by Mark Twain. Copyright, 1924 by Clara Gabrilowitsch. Reprinted by permission of Harper & Row, Publishers, Inc. "A Tale From the Pennsylvania Dutch Country" abridged and adapted from p. 2 and abridged from p. XV "Introduction" in *The New Pennsylvania Dutch Cook Book* by Ruth Hutchison. Copyright ©1958 by Ruth Shepherd Hutchison. Reprinted by permission of Harper & Row, Publishers, Inc. Excerpt ("There is no spectacle...") from p. 443 in *The Web and the Rock* by Thomas Wolfe. Copyright, 1937 by Maxwell Perkins as Executor. Reprinted by permission of Harper & Row, Publishers, Inc. and the British publishers, William Heinemann Ltd. "Old Wives' Tales" reprinted with permission from *Superstitions* by Frederick Heider. Copyright ©1969 by Frederick Heider. "Mushrooms for Breakfast" from *The Good Fare and Cheer of Old England* by Joan Parry Dutton. Copyright ©1960 by Joan Parry Dutton. Reprinted by permission of William Morrow & Co., Inc. and Curtis Brown, Ltd. "Nature's Garden" from *Stalking the Good Life* by Euell Gibbons. Copyright ©1971 by Euell Gibbons. Published by David McKay Company, Inc. Reprinted with permission. Excerpt from *The Horizon Cookbook* by William Harlan Hale. ©1968, American Heritage Publishing Company, Inc. Reprinted by permission of McGraw-Hill Book Company, Inc. "At Delmonico's" from *Delmonico's — A Century of Splendor* by Lately Thomas. Copyright ©1967 by Houghton Mifflin Company. Reprinted by permission of the publisher, Houghton Mifflin Company. "Potatoes, Everyone?" and "Queen Elizabeth I Pays a Visit" from the book *Tales of the Table* by Barbara Norman. ©1972 by Barbara Norman. Published by Prentice-Hall, Inc., Englewood Cliffs, New Jersey. Reprinted by permission of Prentice-Hall, Inc. and Robert P. Mills Limited. "A Rationless Rendezvous" from *Food and Other Frailties* by Romilly Fedden. ©Seeley, Service & Co. Ltd. Reprinted by permission. "Christmas in Germany" from *The German Cookbook*, by Mimi Sheraton. Copyright ©1965 by Mimi Sheraton. Reprinted by permission of Random House, Inc. and Collins-Knowlton-Wing, Inc. "The Origins of Beer" and "The World of Human Needs" from *Food in History* by Reay Tannahill. Copyright ©1973 by Reay Tannahill. Reprinted with permission of Stein and Day/Publishers and Eyre Methuen Ltd./Publishers. "A Snack! A Snack!" reprinted by permission of Charles Scribner's Sons from *Of Time and the River* by Thomas Wolfe. Copyright 1935 Charles Scribner's Sons. "The Bake Sale" from *The Wonderful World of Cooking* by Edward Harris Heth. Copyright ©1956 by Edward Harris Heth. Reprinted by permission of Simon & Schuster, Inc., Publisher. "The Elephant Cutlet" from *La Bonne Table* by Ludwig Bemelmans. Copyright ©1964 by Simon & Schuster, Inc. Reprinted by permission of Simon & Schuster, Inc., Publisher. "Chop Suey" from *The Pleasures of Chinese Cooking* by Grace Zia Chu. Copyright ©1962 by Grace Zia Chu. Reprinted by permission of Simon & Schuster, Inc., Publisher. "Cuisine and Culture" from *The Art of Eating* by M. F. K. Fisher. Copyright ©1954 by M. F. K. Fisher. Reprinted by permission of Russell & Volkening, Inc. "Pasta!" by Marcella Hazan reprinted by permission from the November 16, 1974, issue of *Saturday Review/World*. Copyright ©1974 by Saturday Review/World, Inc. "Morning Prayer" reprinted by permission from George Webb, *A Pima Remembers*, Tucson: University of Arizona Press, copyright 1959. "Eating Out" from *Crowds and Power* by Elias Canetti, translated by Carol Stewart. ©English translation: Victor Gollancz Ltd., 1962. Reprinted by permission of The Viking Press, Inc. and Victor Gollancz Ltd.

©1976, Hallmark Cards, Inc., Kansas City, Missouri.
Printed in the United States of America.
Library of Congress Catalog Card Number: 75-13016.
Standard Book Number: 87529-455-3.

# INTRODUCTION

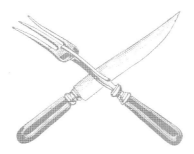

"The pleasure of the table belongs to all ages, to all conditions, to all countries and to all eras; it mingles with all other pleasures, and remains at last to console us for their departure." Such was the ever-green wisdom of Brillat-Savarin, an eighteenth-century French lawyer and gourmet. And such is the fidelity of food. We have all been blessed by its mercurial magic, its memory and anticipation. Pinnacles of childhood are recalled at the instant remembrance of some tantalizing treat. A disabled, love-sick heart has often, in a moment, been nourished into forgetfulness. The significant ghosts of yesterday survive, not in the mind's eye, but in the persistent palate.

Food is the theme of this book. Its variations and recurrences are ancient and modern; poem and song; seasons and seasoning; oysters and elephants; bread, wine and cheese; royalty and peasants; religion and survival; French, English and American; literature, love and romance. It knows no boundaries. The summing up is Thackeray's: "Next to eating good dinners, a healthy man with a benevolent turn of mind must like, I think, to read about them."

And so, **The Romance of Food** is served — a feast of words and pictures. It contains some helpings of history, along with many a morsel of wit and wisdom. It is a varied repast, a savory sampling from the universal table: in short, a delicious book. Bon appetit!

## GRACE

*Elizabethan grace before meals.*

For bread and salt, for grapes and malt,
For flesh and fish, and every dish:
Mutton and beefe, of all meates cheefe:
For cow-heels, chitterlings, tripes and souse,
And other meate that's in the house:
For backs, for brests, for legges, for loines,
For pies with raisons, and with proines:
For fritters, pancakes, and for freyes,
For venison pasties, and minc't pies:
Sheephead and garlick, brawne and mustard,
Wafers, spic'd cakes, tart and custard,
For capons, rabets, pigges and geese,
For apples, carawaies and cheese:
For all these and many moe
Benedicamus Domino.

*Anthelme Brillat-Savarin, whose name is nearly synonymous with the art of eating, left us his legacy in* The Physiology of Taste. *A critic had this to say about the famous book: "There are not only the clearness and elegance and felicity which are impressed on all good French writing, but his style is also so cheerful and picturesque that it positively smiles...." So here are some thoughts from Brillat-Savarin to set the mood for what follows.*

But for life the universe were nothing, and all that has life requires nourishment.

Animals feed, man eats; the man of sense and culture alone understands eating.

The fate of nations depends upon how they are fed.

Tell me what you eat, and I will tell you what you are.

In compelling man to eat that he may live, Nature gives appetite to invite him, and pleasure to reward him.

It is only at table that a man never feels bored during the first hour.

The discovery of a new dish does more for the happiness of the human race than the discovery of a planet.

A drunkard knows not how to drink, and he who eats too much, or too quickly, knows not how to eat.

In eating, the order is from the more substantial to the lighter.

To maintain that a man must not change his wine is a heresy: the palate becomes cloyed, and, after three or four glasses, it is but a deadened sensation that even the best wine provokes.

In a cook, the most essential quality is punctuality; it should also be that of the guest.

It is a breach of politeness towards guests who are punctual when they are kept waiting for one who is late.

He who receives friends without himself bestowing some pains upon the repast prepared for them, does not deserve to have friends.

To receive anyone as our guest is to become responsible for his happiness during the whole time he is under our roof.

## HOSTMANSHIP

*Mrs. Martha Bradley*
The British Housewife, *1770*

In the Old Times in England People thought they never entertained one another well if they did not feed them till they almost burst; as at present a Man in Germany never thinks he makes much of another if he do not make him drunk: But this is a Custom set aside for a much more reasonable Civility....

As our Grandmothers made too much Racket with their Guests: we are in danger of making too little; so natural it is for Ladies to run from one Extreme to another: Those good old Gentlewomen were always finding Fault with their Food, and thought they shewed their own Skill in letting their Company know what was amiss, and their Civility in expressing their Concern that Things were not good enough for their Entertainment: On the other Hand, our Ladies are apt to neglect the Thing entirely; they take no Notice of their Provision; it goes as it comes, and the Company have no Way to know they are welcome but by remembering they were asked.

A middle Practice is better: Let the truly polite Lady take some Notice of the Things, though not too much, and let her praise a Dish that is good tho' 'tis her own; 'tis civil to recommend it to her Company.

# A SOUP SONG

*Lewis Carroll*

The Mock Turtle sighed deeply, and began in a voice sometimes
choked with sobs, to sing this:

> "Beautiful Soup, so rich and green,
>   Waiting in a hot tureen!
>   Who for such dainties would not stoop?
>   Soup of the evening, beautiful Soup!
>   Soup of the evening, beautiful Soup!
>
>     Beau — ootiful Soo — oop!
>     Beau — ootiful Soo — oop!
>   Soo — oop of the e — e — evening,
>     Beautiful, beautiful Soup!
>
>   Beautiful Soup! Who cares for fish,
>   Game, or any other dish?
>   Who would not give all else for two
>   Pennyworth only of beautiful Soup?
>   Pennyworth only of beautiful Soup?
>     Beau — ootiful Soo — oop!
>     Beau — ootiful Soo — oop!
>   Soo — oop of the e — e — evening,
>     Beautiful, beauti — FUL SOUP!"

## THE PEACEMAKER

*From a letter written by John Keats, 1819*

I never drink above three glasses of wine, and never any spirits and water; though, by the bye, the other day Woodhouse took me to his coffee-house, and ordered a bottle of claret. How I like claret! when I can get claret, I must drink it. 'Tis the only palate affair that I am at all sensual in. Would it not be a good spec. to send you some vine-roots? Could it be done? I'll inquire. If you could make some wine like claret, to drink on summer evenings in an arbor! It fills one's mouth with a gushing freshness, then goes down cool and feverless: then, you do not feel it quarreling with one's liver. No; 'tis rather a peacemaker and lies as quiet as it did in the grape.

## FOR THY STOMACH'S SAKE

*William Turner, from the first book on wines in English*

Some use wine for profit, some to make them merry withal, and some for pleasure, and some for all these purposes. Wine doth not only nourish, but maketh the meats to go well down, and stirreth up the natural heat and increaseth it.... But if a man will use it wisely, it will digest or distribute the nourishment, increase the blood and nourish; it will also make the mind both gentler and bolder.

## MORSELS

There is no love sincerer
than the love of food.

*Shaw*

# THE ALGONQUIN

*Gertrude Athearton*

Strangers visit all the de luxe restaurants as a matter of routine, but —
if they can get a table — they lunch at least once at the Algonquin to
gaze upon the celebrities that gather not only about the Round Table
but in groups of twos and fours all over the spacious room.

I myself have seen there at various times Hergesheimer, Edna
St. Vincent Millay, John Emerson and Anita Loos, Heywood Broun,
Carl Van Vechten and Fania Marinoff, Irvin Cobb, Douglas
Fairbanks and Mary Pickford, John Barrymore, George Jean Nathan,
Alexander Woollcott, Scott Fitzgerald, Charles Hanson Towne, Gladys
Unger, Hendrik van Loon. Once I took Rebecca West there for lunch
and she was a source of lively interest on both sides of the rope.

# THE ALGONQUIN AGAIN

*O. O. McIntyre*

I think of all the lures of the Algonquin, its supremest is its old-
fashioned strawberry shortcake. Mesdames et messieurs, there is a
dish! I am by the way of being a shortcake boy. There are few
versions of it I have not tasted from the atrocity at Shepheard's in
Cairo to the exquisite yum-yum turned out by the Frontenac in
Quebec.

Yet not one comes within 10 city blocks of the Algonquin brand.
You have a feeling that whoever has fashioned it has done so in the
spirit of love. And thus does it become somehow a poem of ardour.
It's swell.

# PASTA!

*Italian expert Marcella Hazan, author of* The Classic Italian Cookbook, *provides these descriptions of packaged pastas properly called* macaroni *in America. Her complete repertoire includes an equally long, palate-pleasing list of pastas made by hand at home.*

If Scheherazade had been an Italian girl, she wouldn't have had to tell stories. She could have won her daily reprieve by plying the sultan with a different and delectable dish of pasta for 1,001 nights, or for every night of his life if it had been necessary. Italian regional cooking boasts more than 60,000 clearly recognized different dishes — not including an unnumbered host of individual variations — and a notable part of this astonishing repertory consists of a confusing variety of pastas. It is unlikely that man's inventiveness has ever been poured out in larger measure on any other single group of artifacts.

Pasta is made in dozens of different shapes, each of which is multiplied by variations in size, thickness, and surface texture. As pasta changes size and shape, it develops differences in character so that each type requires a suitable cooking procedure and a uniquely compatible set of sauces....

This brief glossary does not intend to settle or to stir any great etymological controversy. Its objective is to give some useful descriptions, to show that the world of pasta can be infinitely more interesting and varied than most people suspect, and to encourage readers to strike out exploring on their own.

---

**Bucatini.** Also known as Perciatelli. It is a thicker, hollow version of spaghetti. Its most famous preparation originated in Amatrice, near Rome. *Bucatini all'Amatriciana* is served with a sauce made of rendered pork fat (or butter), pork jowl (or *pancetta*, Italian bacon), tomatoes, hot red pepper, and *pecorino romano* cheese.

---

**Conchiglie.** Means "seashells." This variety of pasta resembles those rounded shells that are pinched at both ends, have a long, narrow opening, and are sometimes used in necklaces or bracelets. It comes either ridged or smooth, and its cavity is ideal for trapping meat sauces or sauces made with ham and peas or crumbled sausages and cream.

**Fusilli.** A spiral version of spaghetti. Also called, in slightly different forms, Tortiglioni or Rotelle. This shape is particularly well suited to clinging, thick, creamy sauces containing bits of sausage or ham or vegetables, such as zucchini. It does not go well with loose tomato or oil-based sauces.

**Pastina.** A general term for a whole variety of tiny pasta shapes, such as *anellini, stellette, ditalini,* and others. It is best served with a good homemade meat broth and topped with freshly grated Parmesan cheese.

**Penne.** Means "quills" and is shaped somewhat like a very broad, diagonally truncated quill. It is usually smooth, although there are also ridged "quills," Penne Rigate. The classic accompaniment for *penne* is a light, briefly simmered sauce of tomatoes and butter.

**Rigatoni.** A stubby, hollow, slightly curved, ridged tubular macaroni. It is ideal with meat-and-cheese sauces. Because it maintains its firmness longer than most macaroni does, it is often first boiled, drained, and sauced, then topped with béchamel and baked.

**Spaghetti.** Thin, solid strings whose thickness determines how it is served. Thin spaghetti, or Spaghettini, usually tastes best with oil-based sauces containing clams, mussels, or other seafood or such vegetables as eggplant and zucchini. One of the most satisfying and fastest preparations for *spaghettini* is *ajo e ojo,* olive oil with sautéed garlic. Spaghetti, on the other hand, has a special affinity for butter and cheese and tomato sauces. Though spaghetti can be served with ham and peas or bacon and cheese or crumbled sausages and cream, it is hardly, if ever, served with meat sauce and certainly never with meatballs. In Naples and other parts of the south, spaghetti and spaghettini are sometimes known as *vermicelli* and *vermicellini*.

**Ziti.** Basically a smaller, smooth-surfaced version of *rigatoni*. Like *rigatoni*, it is often served baked.

---

## MOROCCO

*Rupert Croft-Cooke*

Morocco is hardly a gourmet's paradise — for either its raw materials or its cooking methods — but there are delicious and interesting things in both categories. The appeal is to the sight and smell as much as to the taste. The food markets, flashing with brilliant color, are unforgettable. The Berber women in scarlet-and-white striped skirts and straw hats wider than Mexican sombreros sit beside their piles of variegated fruits and vegetables: purple eggplants, deep-red peppers, oranges, bananas, and the rest. Flower stalls sell the incredible wild flowers of the country — iris *tingitana,* the scented wild narcissus, wild asphodel, and mountains of mimosa blooms.

As for the culinary smells — who can forget walking through the narrow passages of the medina or native quarter and being drawn to an open-fronted restaurant where *pinchitos* or kebabs are grilled over charcoal, the juices dripping and sizzling on the embers and sending up savory smoke to scent the evening air? Or the cry of *"Yeo!"* from small boys who pass among the dwellings with trays on their heads, collecting flattish piles of dough that will be baked in the communal oven? That sound is as natural and timeless as the cry of the muezzin from the mosque.

## THE WORLD OF HUMAN NEEDS

*Reay Tannahill*

A very fair picture of the important elements in the Indian diet is given in the *Puranas*, or "Ancient Stories," a curious compilation of legend, religious instruction, and obscure geographical information dating from somewhere in the early centuries of the present era.

The human world, it was said, formed a series of concentric circles around Mount Meru — a succession of ring-like continents separated from one another by seven oceans. The ocean immediately surrounding Mount Meru was composed of salt; the next of *jaggeri*, a very coarse, sticky, dark brown sugar; the third of wine; the fourth of *ghi* (boiled and clarified butter); the fifth of milk; the sixth of curds; and the seventh of fresh water.

Of these seven magical oceans, representing the staple needs of mankind in India (other than grain), no less than three were of dairy products.

## SCRIPTURE CAKE

*Amy Atkinson and Grace Holroyd*

1. 4½ cups of Kings iv. 22 v.
2. 1½ cups of Judges v. 25 v.
3. 2 cups of Jeremiah vi. 20 v.
4. 2 cups of I Samuel xxv. 18 v.
5. 2 cups of Nahum iii. 12 v.
6. 1 cup of Numbers xvii. 8 v.
7. 2 tablespoonsful I Samuel xiv. 25 v.
8. Season to taste II Chronicles ix. 9 v.
9. 6 cups Jeremiah xvii. 11 v.
10. 1 pinch Leviticus ii. 13 v.
11. 1 cup of Judges iv. 19 last clause.
12. 3 teaspoonsful Amos iv. 5 v.
13. Follow Solomon's prescription for the making of a good boy and you will have a good cake, see Proverbs xxiii. 14 v.

# THE BAKE SALE

*Edward Harris Heth*

Autumn continues over the woods and valley like a great, slow illumination. Strangely in these days of cessation, the light grows brighter. You can see far distances, and everywhere trees and hills are glinted with the red afterglow of summer. These are reposeful days. But in the village there is no such repose. One of these days a homemade sign will probably appear in the post office:

BAKe SALe · Proceeds To P.T.A. · SAT. 10 A.m.

And SAT. 10 A.M. presents more hazards than one would think. The bake sale, held in the post office or rear of the grocery store or sometimes in the fire station, has aspects of slaughter about it. Every house in the village harbors children, hence every parent belongs to the P.T.A. and in each of these houses for the past few days there has been a chopping of nuts and rolling of dough and scraping of bowls, and the yeasty fragrance of homemade breads and rolls and kuchen.

This is the proper season for baking — wasps buzzing dizzily in last flecks of autumn sunlight, children rattling in leaf piles, the days slower in pace and growing nippy. Ovens that have been grudgingly lighted only when necessary during the sweltering months now are lit with a pop of joy that relief has come. The comfortable baking days are here again and the women visit each other in their warm kitchens; the moment the baked goods are taken from the oven, they sit right down at their kitchen tables to sample them, hot and steaming, along with a cup of coffee.

On the morning of the sale the members of the P.T.A. have already congregated by eight o'clock, baskets and suit boxes heavy with their breads and cookies and biscuits. These are carefully spread on long tables overlaid with neat white paper, Mrs. Gardner's nut cake and Aunt Dell's rich rolls and Erna Mason's plum cake all displayed on paper doilies as grandly as in a Fifth Avenue confiserie window. All this behind locked doors, remember, the ladies carrying on like a meeting of the Gestapo. Then, once their wares are arranged, they swiftly start buying the cakes and breads from each other and sometimes even their own tortes; by the time the doors are unlocked at ten o'clock to admit the public (which I have come to conclude consists only of myself, childless, hence barred from the P.T.A.), there is nothing left to buy.

I reach out toward a pan of redolent golden muffins that seem still to be smoking only to have a small black cloth coin purse (of the kind my mother called her pocketbook) rapped sharply against my wrist. "Unh-unh," the lady smiles with unwonted fiendishness, "I've spoken for those. All bought and paid for. Sorry." I reach for a streusel coffeecake contributed by Mary Soderman only to have it whisked out of my fingertips into a black oilcloth shopping bag which I recognize as Mrs. Jeffke's. All the women look satisfied and there is a great deal of laughter. But man cannot live on laughter alone.

The air is tantalizing with the odors of yeast and flour and cleanliness and jams hidden inside doughnuts and warmth and the prickly sweetness of baked sugar and contented talk. Now, at four minutes past ten o'clock, the women are already closing up shop, busy exchanging favorite recipes as they leave.

## MORSELS

When mighty roast beef was England's food,
It ennobled our hearts, and enriched our blood;
Our soldiers were brave and our courtiers were good.
Oh! The roast beef of England.

*Richard Leveridge*

# POTATOES, EVERYONE?

*Barbara Norman*

*Some foods we consider commonplace today were once shrouded in mystery and fear. One of these is the tomato, or "love apple," which was thought to be poisonous for more than two centuries after its discovery in America.*

*Other unfamiliar edibles were rejected simply for reasons of taste. Here is an account of an eighteenth-century public relations campaign that finally brought the potato into favor in France.*

The man who finally made potatoes accepted in France was an apothecary named Parmentier (the culinary term "parmentier" today means prepared or served with potatoes). After living almost exclusively on potatoes for a year while a prisoner in Prussia during the Seven Years' War, Parmentier decided the potato would improve the French diet. He met savage opposition. Accused of trying to force his "pig fodder" on the pensioners, he was forced to resign from the post of pharmacist at the Hôtel des Invalides. Parmentier's opportunity came in 1769, when the town of Besancon held a contest for the plant that would make the best substitute for grain cereals in time of famine. The jury gave Parmentier's potato first prize. Parmentier was asked to travel through France to study the poor quality of bread and recommend changes. Like most Europeans, he thought of the potato as a source of flour rather than a vegetable. In it he saw the possibility of cheap, nutritious bread for everyone. Parmentier was the first to work out a recipe for making bread from potatoes without the addition of cereal flour, but his idea was never adopted.

Undiscouraged, Parmentier continued to believe in the usefulness and versatility of the potato. He invited some prominent friends, including Benjamin Franklin, to a dinner composed entirely of potatoes prepared in twenty different ways. He began growing potatoes on sixty-odd acres of poor land the French government let him use to prove the new vegetable would grow in bad soil. To arouse public curiosity, he arranged to have the field conspicuously guarded by soldiers by day but not by night, when, as he anticipated, the field was systematically robbed by people eager to try so valuable a food. On August 25, 1785, Parmentier brought a potato-flower bouquet to

Louis XVI on the occasion of the royal birthday and had the satisfaction of hearing the King announce that thanks to the potato there would be no more famine. Marie Antoinette pinned on a potato flower, Louis XVI put one in his buttonhole, Parmentier did likewise, and the courtiers were so eager to follow suit that some paid as much as ten louis for a single flower. Nevertheless it took the hard times of the French Revolution and the famine of 1816 for the potato to be generally accepted.

# A FEAST OF NATIONS

*Alpheus Hyatt Verrill*

All corners of the world supply our meals. There are lentils from France in our soups, we nibble olives from Spain, and eat sardines from Portugal or Norway. The oil of our salad-dressing may come from Italy. The almonds of our dessert were gathered in Greece and the figs were picked in far-off Arabia. There is caviar from Russia, tea from India and China, rice from Japan or perhaps from Siam or the Philippines; spices from Borneo, Sumatra and the Celebes. We use cheese from Holland or Switzerland, marmalade from England, kippers from Scotland and Scandinavia. We drink coffee from Brazil, Colombia and Central America, and cocoa and chocolate from Ecuador, Peru, Trinidad and Africa. We enjoy grapefruit from Puerto Rico, Cuba, Florida and California, and oranges from the same sources. From the towering mountain sides of the Lesser Antilles come our limes; Mexico supplies many of our melons, and there are grapes, cherries and other fruits from Chile and the Argentine. We eat onions from Cuba, potatoes from Bermuda, tomatoes from the Bahamas, with countless other viands from far and near. Even the unfathomable depths of the oceans supply us with many kinds of fish. The naked Indians of tropical jungles, and the natives of Java contribute the tapioca for our puddings, while the nuts from waving palm trees on many a tropic isle go into our cakes, pies and candies.

## MORSELS

And we meet, with champagne
and chicken, at last!

*Lady Mary Wortley Montago*

## THE BREAD OF LIFE

*John 6:24-35*

When the people therefore saw that Jesus was not there, neither his disciples, they also took shipping, and came to Capernaum, seeking for Jesus. And when they had found him on the other side of the sea, they said unto him, Rabbi, when camest thou hither? Jesus answered them and said, Verily, verily, I say unto you, Ye seek me, not because ye saw the miracles, but because ye did eat of the loaves, and were filled. Labour not for the meat which perisheth, but for that meat which endureth unto everlasting life, which the Son of man shall give unto you: for him hath God the Father sealed.

Then said they unto him, What shall we do, that we might work the works of God? Jesus answered and said unto them, This is the work of God, that ye believe on him whom he hath sent. They said therefore unto him, What sign shewest thou then, that we may see, and believe thee? what dost thou work? Our fathers did eat manna in the desert; as it is written, He gave them bread from heaven to eat. Then Jesus said unto them, Verily, verily, I say unto you, Moses gave you not that bread from heaven; but my Father giveth you the true bread from heaven. For the bread of God is he which cometh down from heaven, and giveth life unto the world.

Then said they unto him, Lord, evermore give us this bread. And Jesus said unto them, I am the bread of life: he that cometh to me shall never hunger; and he that believeth on me shall never thirst.

## BIBLE BITES

Man doth not live by bread only. — *Deuteronomy*

---

A man hath no better thing under the sun,
than to eat, and to drink and to be merry. — *Ecclesiastes*

---

Give us this day our daily bread. — *Matthew*

---

# IN THE GOOD OLD SUMMERTIME

*Mark Twain*

In the summer the table was set in the middle of that shady and breezy floor, and the sumptuous meals — well, it makes me cry to think of them. Fried chicken, roast pig, wild and tame turkeys, ducks and geese, venison just killed, squirrels, rabbits, pheasants, partridges, prairie-chickens; biscuits, hot batter-cakes, hot buckwheat cakes, hot "wheat bread," hot rolls, hot cornpone; fresh corn boiled on the ear, succotash, butter-beans, string-beans, tomatoes, peas, Irish potatoes, sweet potatoes; buttermilk, sweet milk; "clabber"; watermelons, muskmelons, cantaloupes — all fresh from the garden — apple pie, peach pie, pumpkin pie, apple dumplings, peach cobbler — I can't remember the rest.

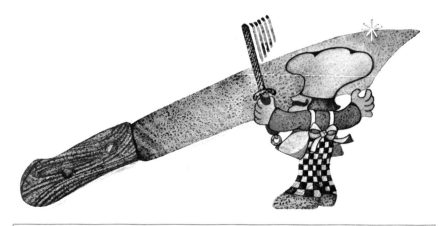

## THE ELEPHANT CUTLET

*Ludwig Bemelmans*

Once upon a time there were two men in Vienna who wanted to open a restaurant. One was a dentist who was tired of fixing teeth and always wanted to own a restaurant, and the other a famous cook by the name of Souphans.

The dentist was, however, a little afraid. "There are," he said, "already too many restaurants in Vienna, restaurants of every kind, Viennese, French, Italian, Chinese, American, American-Chinese, Portuguese, Armenian, Dietary, Vegetarian, Jewish, Wine and Beer restaurants — in short, all sorts of restaurants."

But the chef had an Idea. "There is one kind of restaurant that Vienna has not," he said.

"What kind?" said the dentist.

"A restaurant such as has never existed before, a restaurant for cutlets from every animal in the world."

The dentist was afraid, but finally he agreed, and the famous chef went out to buy a house, tables and chairs, and engaged help, pots and pans and had a sign painted with big red letters ten feet high saying:

# "CUTLETS FROM EVERY ANIMAL IN THE WORLD"

The first customer that entered the door was a distinguished lady, a countess. She sat down and asked for an elephant cutlet.

"How would Madame like this elephant cutlet cooked?" said the waiter.

"Oh, Milanaise, sauté in butter, with a little spaghetti over it, on that a filet of anchovy, and an olive on top," she said.

"That is very nice," said the waiter and went out to order it.

"Jessas Maria und Joseph!" said the dentist when he heard the order, and he turned to the chef and cried, "What did I tell you? Now what are we going to do?"

The chef said nothing; he put on a clean apron and walked into the dining room to the table of the lady. There he bowed, bent down to her and said, "Madame has ordered an elephant cutlet?"

"Yes," said the countess.

"With spaghetti and a filet of anchovy and an olive?"

"Yes."

"Madame is all alone?"

"Yes, yes."

"Madame expects no one else?"

"No."

"And Madame wants only one cutlet?"

"Yes," said the lady, "but why all these questions?"

"Because," said the chef, "because, Madame, I am very sorry, but for one cutlet we cannot cut up our elephant."

# MUSHROOMS FOR BREAKFAST

*Joan Parry Dutton*

Mushrooms for breakfast! As I write those words my Aunt Mary's kitchen at Ladye Grove, just across the fields from Birley, my father's old home in Herefordshire, comes clear as a color slide before my eyes. I imagine a crisp autumn morning, waiting as the clock on the wall ticked slowly but surely toward the nine o'clock breakfast, sniffing the smell of mushrooms and bacon sizzling in the frying pan....

Mushrooming is a country game of chance. The common mushrooms are choosey, and a likely looking field may prove barren, or some earlier bird may have stolen a march on you. There is a tradition, as I well remember from sleepy-eyed experience, that to get any mushrooms at all you should be up at dawn. This is nonsense.

The best time to gather mushrooms is in the early evening up to twilight, when the dew is on the grass, and the whiteness of a flower or feather, or even a head of thistledown, may trick you on and on across the meadow in the fading light. But oh, to find, to bend down and pick this fragile, beautiful meadow mushroom; to feel its satin-smooth white umbrella top and see the lining, crinkled pink, beneath; to have for a moment the fragrance of damp autumn earth in the hollow of your hand! To come home in the dusk with a basket of mushrooms on your arm!

Many an evening as a girl I sat on the edge of the kitchen table, my tired legs dangling, never too tired to help prepare the mushrooms I had found for the next morning's breakfast. We peeled the skins, removed the stems, and spread them out on a dish. Then we seasoned them with pepper and salt, and set them to stand overnight in the cool larder. Invariably you are advised to grill mushrooms in melted butter, or stew them in milk, but our way was simply to fry them with bacon until they swam in their black fragrant juice. That is the old way; the poacher's, the shepherd's, the gypsy's way — the only way.

# CUISINE AND CULTURE

*Cuisine, or the art of preparing food in a distinctive style, began nearly as far back in time as eating itself. Its origins are as mysterious and diverse as the origins of mankind, and its forms are as rich as culture.*

*M. F. K. Fisher provides this overview of taste, as it were, as it developed in various parts of the civilized world, from the imperial courts of China to the banquet halls of Rome.*

Twenty-eight hundred years before Jesus broke bread for his children, a wise emperor in China thought of his. Shennung was his name, and before he died he had compiled a great cookbook, the *Hon-Zo*. In forty-seven centuries we have not learned much more about food than it can tell.

While Shennung's millions died and lived, humans all over this world were eating according to their fashions, but principally because they had to. From the north still came a faint snarl of hungry blond men gnashing at raw meat.... But all around the Mediterranean and to the east, a ring of good things was sprouting. Gradually fig trees were planted, and then grapes, and wheat grew because men made it. New pleasures were born for the warm brown people....

Whispers and odours and the tantalizing noises of banqueting floated swiftly westward. Greece heard and smelled and was fascinated. Gastronomy nourished itself on rumour, and from the Spartan black broth was born a refined and decadent philosophy of eating.

In their love for fresh vegetables and native fruits, however, the Greeks kept their cuisine basically simple. Honey they used for all sweetening, leaving the cane sugar brought from China to the medicine-makers. Chestnuts were roasted, as they had been for centuries, and eaten after meals with dried fruits.

But now delicate little cakes of sesame and honey were served at the same time, and cities became rivals in varying their shapes and flavors....

Locusts were still roasted a light golden hue, and meats spitted over coals, but with a new, investigating fervour. Peacocks were served in their feathers. Pork, long the favourite viand, was found to have over fifty different flavours!

And fish, that long-known flesh for soups and stews, emerged from monotony with a whole complex science of its own. Sole was the king of all the dishes, but almost every swimming creature was cooked at one time or another.

The Greeks drank their own wines, and those not naturally sweet they flavoured to cloying heaviness with honey and aromatic herbs and spices. Their *hippocras*, which was just such a syrupy punch, became after several centuries the favourite drink of France's fourteenth Louis.

As the art of eating grew in Greece, men began to write about it. Artimidorus Aristophanius left recipes, some of them very strange to us and as often generous of good suggestions. More than one modern cook has tried his method of using sour young grapes instead of vinegar, and has been well pleased....

While Greece exchanged black broth and its accompanying simplicity for that more complex kitchen science nurtured by her new esthetes, Rome shadowed her some years behind, mimicking with fantastic exaggeration each of her calm inevitable developments.

For her Spartan pottage, Romans had a gruel of lentils. They too ate chestnuts and cheeses and fruits and green vegetables, with honey to sweeten and wine to gladden. Then when refinement, sure arbiter of a decadent civilization, crept into the Grecian cuisine, her tardy shadow Rome leaped feverishly in a grotesque and fascinating imitation.

As had happened in Greece, town and villages vied for culinary honours. Certain cakes, cheeses of a special smell, and even fish from a named lake or river began to cause small feuds among the gourmets. Gradually shadow out-leaped self, and in their furious delicacy of palate and heavy-handed subtlety of selection the wealthy Romans left Greeks far behind.

Are *pâtés de foie gras* better made from cygnets than from milk-white geese? Of course! Not at all! Well, perhaps if the geese are nourished solely on green figs — But on the other hand, a diet of almonds —

Senators cut important electors in the streets; sons quarrelled with fathers, boys with their tutors. Even the philosophers considered such questions weightily, and uttered decisions which had but temporary effect.

When Cleopatra melted her pearl and six million sesterces into the world's most expensive recipe, she set a tantalizingly high mark.

Until Rome fell, gourmets tried to outdo her. Undoubtedly the results were more palatable – but never more costly....

It was Lucullus who sorted his friends into different rooms, rather like the various restaurants in a large German railroad station. In some rooms, a meal cost only one or two hundred dollars for each person. Decoration there was relatively simple. More expensive surroundings showed that here Lucullus spent more on his food.

And finally, in the Apollo Room, where only his very intimate or important guests were invited, he spent one thousand dollars for each person....

Other men blinked at their own banquet bills, or complained bitterly, like Julius Caesar when he found he had spent five millions sterling, one Roman summer, on suppers for his friends – and on barley water mixed with wine, for his favourite charger to drink from a golden trough!

## THE ORIGINS OF BEER

*Reay Tannahill*

Greek tradition has it that the god Dionysus fled from Mesopotamia in disgust because its people were so addicted to beer....

Beer preparation may first have evolved from a particular method of breadmaking. The neolithic housewife had learned how to make raw grain digestible by leaving it to sprout. But she had gone on to discover that bread made from sprouted grain which had been dried and then pounded kept better than bread made from conventional flour, and by the early Egyptian period beer-making was specifically related not to raw sprouted grain but to baked bread. A special dough was made from sprouted, dried grains, and partially baked; the "loaves" were then broken up and put to soak in water; and the mixture was allowed to ferment for about a day. After this, the liquor was strained off and the beer was ready to drink. By the end of the third millennium B.C., Egyptian brewers were making differently spiced and flavored "beer breads" and their customers had a correspondingly wide range of brews to choose from.

# UP AND DOWN

*Margaret Powell*

*Here is a view of daily life from "below stairs" during that grand era in England known as Edwardian. Then, household politics vied with national politics as a matter of interest, intrigue and protocol. And social position was reflected in all facets of life, including the kinds of food consumed upstairs and down.*

The amount of food that came into that house seemed absolutely fabulous to me, the amount of food that was eaten and wasted too. They often had a whole saddle of mutton. You don't see saddles very much now but they were gorgeous things. And sirloins. Sometimes with the sirloin they would only eat the undercut and the whole top was left over, so we used to have that for our dinner. Even so, we couldn't eat everything and a lot got thrown away. When I used to think of my family at home where we seldom had enough to eat, it used to break my heart.

The milkman called three times a day — at half past four to five in the morning he would leave some milk, then he would come round again at ten o'clock with more milk and any other orders that you wanted. Naturally he carried cream and eggs with him, but if you wanted butter or cakes which he sold, or anything like that, he came yet again at about two o'clock in the afternoon.

I've never seen such milk and cream and eggs. Pints of cream nearly every day was nothing in that household, even when they weren't entertaining, when there was only Mr. and Mrs. Clydesdale and the young daughter and the governess....

Lunch, according to Mrs. McIlroy, was a very simple meal. Soup, fish, cutlets or a grill, and a sweet. One of the things she taught me was how a dish should be sent up. For instance, when it was cutlets, she would mash the potatoes and roll them in egg and breadcrumbs, in little balls, slightly larger than walnuts, and then she would arrange them in a pyramid on a silver dish and the cutlets would stand on end all round with a little white frill on each bone and parsley at intervals around the dish. It really looked most attractive.

For us the main meal was the middle-day meal because at night we just had anything that was left over. Although it was our main meal I noticed we never got three courses, we only had meat and sweet; fairly substantial, but not cutlets or fillet steak or anything like that. When it was fish, it was herrings or cod. Still, there was always enough of it, and as I'd never been used to luxurious living, I always ate anything there was.

## LUNCHEON ON THE ROAD

*Guy de Maupassant*

At last, at three o'clock, as they were in the midst of an apparently limitless plain, with not a single village in sight, Boule de Suif stooped quickly, and drew from underneath the seat a large basket covered with a white napkin.

From this she extracted first of all a small earthenware plate and a silver drinking cup, then an enormous dish containing two whole chickens cut into joints and imbedded in jelly. The basket was seen to contain other good things: pies, fruit, dainties of all sorts — provisions, in fine, for a three days' journey, rendering their owner independent of wayside inns. The necks of four bottles protruded from among the food. She took a chicken wing, and began to eat it daintily, together with one of those rolls called in Normandy "Régence."

All looks were directed toward her. An odor of food filled the air, causing nostrils to dilate, mouths to water, and jaws to contract painfully. The scorn of the ladies for this disreputable female grew positively ferocious; they would have liked to kill her, or throw her out of the coach into the snow of the road below.

# CHOP SUEY

*Grace Zia Chu*

One day, so the stories go, a group of Americans (they were either miners or prospectors or cowboys, depending on which version of the story you choose) wandered into a Chinese restaurant. They tried, and were delighted by, those new Chinese dishes called "chop suey." They might have been somewhat less delighted had they known that they had been eating "miscellaneous odds and ends," which is what the words chop suey mean in the Cantonese dialect. In any case, the American discoverers of chop suey soon spread the word, and the dish became firmly established in the New World. The evolution of chop suey was to go on over a span of years. After considerable experimentation, a number of "standard" chop suey dishes won their honored places on Chinese restaurant menus, where they remain now and, perhaps, forever.

## MORSELS

A hungry stomach will not allow its owner
to forget it, whatever his cares and sorrows.

*Homer*

The best sauce for food is hunger
and the best flavoring for drink, thirst.

*Socrates*

# QUEEN ELIZABETH I, PAYS A VISIT

*Barbara Norman*

*Food and feasting have forever been employed for political advantage. In simpler times, the powerful presided over banquets to curry favor and to keep the "constituency" fat and happy. Nowadays, the political dinner is perhaps more closely allied to the kinds of occasions by which Queen Elizabeth turned the tables on her wealthy subjects, keeping them loyal by keeping them poor.*

Queen Elizabeth was as eager a traveler as Charles IX. Some historians suspect that not a few of the Queen's visits to her more powerful subjects were designed to ruin them under the pretence of doing them honor. A queenly visit was extremely costly. Each of Queen Elizabeth's not infrequent visits to her principal minister, Lord Burghley, lasted three to six weeks, during which time she held court and received and entertained foreign ambassadors and dignitaries at the expense of her host, who was out two or three thousand pounds every time she did him this honor.

Lord North recorded in his household book the items consumed during the Queen's two-day visit to his estate at Kirtling in 1577:

10,000  loaves of bread
    74  hogsheads of beer, 2 tons of ale, 7 hogsheads of wine, 20 gallons of sack, 6 gallons of hippocras
    12  steers and oxen

      67  sheep, 7 lambs, 18 calves, 34 pigs
       4  stags and 16 bucks made into 276 pasties
       8  gammons of bacon
     220  neats' tongues, feet, and udders
   4,828  geese, capons, chickens, pigeons, quail, turkeys, swans, cranes,
             and ducks
     559  bitterns, shovelers, pewits, godwits, pulls, dotterels, heronsews,
             cranes, snipe, knots, plover, stints, redshanks, tern, partridge,
             pheasants, and curlews
       3  kegs of sturgeon
       8  dozen crayfish
       1  cartload and 2 horseloads of oysters
       1  barrel of anchovies
     300  red herrings and 18 other fish
     430  pounds of butter and 13 pounds of lard
   2,522  eggs
       1  hogshead of vinegar
       6  Holland cheeses, 10 marchpanes, "Grocery ware, bankett stuff,
             salletts, rootes, and hearbes."

## EATING OUT

*Elias Canetti*

...A certain esteem for each other is clearly evident in all who eat
together. This is already expressed by the fact of their *sharing*.
The food in the common dish before them belongs to all of them
together. Everyone takes some of it and sees that others take some too.
Everyone tries to be fair and not to take advantage of anyone else. The
bond between the eaters is strongest when it is *one* animal they
partake of, one body which they knew as a living unit, or one loaf
of bread....

# CHRISTMAS IN GERMANY

*Mimi Sheraton*

December 25, Christmas Day (Christtag oder erster Weihnachtstag), should be a day that honors the German talent for superb baking. Dozens of kinds of cookies, large and small cakes, fruit breads and sweet yeast breads like Dresden Stollen are all prepared for this day. Families begin baking four weeks ahead of time, during Advent, and by Christmas Eve, homes are richly scented with ginger, cardamom, anise, nutmeg, vanilla — everything, in fact, except frankincense and myrrh, which probably wouldn't taste so good anyway.

# LAND OF THE PILGRIMS' PRIDE

*Sally Smith Booth*

When European colonists first landed in America they found not only Indians, virgin lands, and an alien style of life, but the world's largest outdoor supermarket.

Ducks, geese, and pigeons by the millions filled the skies. Forests abounded with deer, hare, squirrels, and quail. In rivers and on seashores thrived giant shad, eels, mussels, lobsters five feet long, and crabs said to be big enough to feed four men each. Trees hung heavy with wild fruits and berries. Vegetables, such as potatoes, squash, corn, and pumpkin, covered the rolling meadows.

But the prices were high for shopping in America's forests and streams. Nearly half of the Pilgrims in Plymouth Colony died during the first year of settlement, while more than two hundred kinds of edible fish flourished in nearby Massachusetts Bay. To the south, the Jamestown area of Virginia boasted great wild turkeys weighing as much as fifty pounds each, foot-long oysters, and gigantic clams. Yet during the 1609 "Starving Time," nine out of ten pioneers died, and the remainder survived on a daily ration that included a few kernels of parched corn, supplemented by ants, rats, and boot leather.

# A GRAIN OF GENESIS

Then God said, "Let the earth bring forth vegetation; seed-bearing plants and all kinds of fruit trees that bear fruit containing their seed."
And so it was.
Then God said, "Let the waters abound with life, and above the earth let winged creatures fly below the firmament of the heavens."
And so it was.
God also said, "See, I give you every seed-bearing plant of the earth and every tree which has seed-bearing fruit to be your food. To every wild animal of the earth, to every bird of the air, and to every creature that crawls on earth and has the breath of life, I give the green plants for food."
And so it was.

# THE RITE OF HOSPITALITY

*Colin Clair*

Many passages in the Bible offer us information on the food of the Hebrews. It was for the most part plain and frugal fare, for much of the Holy Land was stony, hard and barren. Bread in the form of coarse barley cakes was the staple diet of the peasant and the women of Israel spent much of their time grinding corn and baking.

In the Book of Genesis we find Abraham receiving the envoys of the Lord with the traditional rites of hospitality: "Let a little water, I pray you, be fetched, and wash your feet, and rest yourselves under the tree: and I will fetch a morsel of bread, and comfort ye your hearts." Throughout the Bible bread and food are synonymous terms.

# MORNING PRAYER

*Pima Indians*

Now another day is coming,
Awake from slumber,
Look toward the east,
See the rising of the sun,
Which means another day to toil.
Another day to hunt for meat,
To put the seed in the ground
That the yield might be good,
So our people may not go hungry.
The great Father provided us the sun
To give life to our earth so
That it might give us a good yield.
And that we might see
To hunt our game for meat.
So arise and make use of the day
And do not get in the way
Of the women as they go about
Fixing up the camp and the
Needed task of preparing meals for you.
Many moons, many suns have come and gone
Since our forefathers here on this same ground
Toiled and struggled so that we might
Enjoy life today.
So let us not waste this day.
But get your tools, go out to the field, or
Take down your bow and arrows
And go after the game, so that
Your family will not be in need of meat.
So now I hope you will strive
To make this day the best in your life.

# A SNACK! A SNACK!

*from* Of Time and the River
*By Thomas Wolfe*

What shall it be now? What shall it be? A snack! A snack! — Before we prowl the meadows of the moon to-night, and soak our hearts in the moonlight's magic and the visions of our youth — what shall it be before we prowl the meadows of the moon? Oh, it shall be a snack, a snack — hah! hah! — it shall be nothing but a snack because — hah! hah! — you understand, we are not hungry and it is not well to eat too much before retiring — so we'll just investigate the icebox as we have done so oft at midnight in America — and we are the moon's man, boys — and all that it will be, I do assure you, will be something swift and quick and ready, something instant and felicitous, and quite delicate and dainty — just a snack.

I think — now let me see — h'm now! — well, perhaps I'll have a slice or two of that pink Austrian ham that smells so sweet and pungent and looks so pretty and so delicate there in the crisp garlands of the parsley leaf! — and yes, perhaps, I'll have a slice of this roast beef, as well — h'm now! — yes, I think that's what I'm going to do — say a slice of red rare meat there at the centre — ah-h! there you are! yes, that's the stuff, that does quite nicely, thank you — with just a trifle of that crisp brown crackling there to oil the lips and make its passage easy, and a little of that cold but brown and oh — most — brawny gravy — and, yes, sir! — I think I *will*, now, that it occurs to me, a slice of that plump chicken — some white meat, thank you, at the breast — ah, there it is! — how sweetly doth the noble fowl submit to the swift and keen persuasion of the knife — and now, perhaps, just for our diet's healthy balance, a spoonful of those lima beans, as gay as April and as sweet as butter, a tomato slice or two, a speared forkful of those thin-sliced cucumbers — ah! what a delicate and toothsome pickle they do make — what sorcerer invented them, a little corn perhaps, a bottle of this milk, a pound of butter and that crusty loaf of bread — and even this moon-haunted wilderness were paradise enow — with just a snack — a snack — a snack — !

# AT DELMONICO'S

*Lately Thomas*

Then one day word came from the office that "Diamond Jim" Brady would give a supper to Lillian Russell that evening. Oscar [Oscar Tschirky, renowned Swiss chef at Delmonico's and, later, the Waldorf] served *that* supper himself. As he told it:

"'Diamond Jim' arrived with Miss Russell and four other guests, a dinner of just the right and fashionable size. I will never forget him as he arrived at Delmonico's. Even if I had not known who he was, I would have been impressed. So would anyone else. He carried a cane with a diamond head, wore two diamond rings, a diamond stickpin in his black silk tie…I found him warm, friendly, and jovial."

How much did "Diamond Jim" Brady really eat? His capacity became traditional in New York: reliable witnesses testified to it, and his global paunch was plain evidence of the cavity he had to fill. Dozens of oysters, gallons of orange juice, steaks "smothered in veal chops" were said to be his normal fare. But Oscar Tschirky, whose testimony is worthy of belief, affirmed that although he served Brady many times, both at Delmonico's and at the Waldorf, he never saw him eat other than moderately. "If he was a great eater he must have done his stuffing elsewhere," was Oscar's unequivocal statement. "Every time I waited on him his order was pretty much the same… He would start off with a dozen raw oysters. Then he would usually have a filet mignon with one green vegetable. For dessert there would be either a slice of apple pie or a portion of watermelon if it were in season. His only beverage was orange juice…That was what he ordered the first night I served him at Delmonico's."

But Brady's guests — including the willowy Lillian [Russell] — this was what they devoured, according to Oscar: oysters, soup, fish, entrée, roast, two vegetables, sherbert, game salad, ice cream, cake, and coffee. And though Brady never drank wine, for his guests the choicest vintages flowed without stint.

"I had the surprise and disillusionment of my life," said Oscar of that evening when he saw La Russell tuck into the grub with the determination of a stagehand.

## WORDS FROM THE WISE IN WINE

*Alma Whitaker*

It is told of King Edward VII that he once felt called upon to reprove a Foreign Ambassador at his table.

He had, you see, honored the gentleman by having a peculiarly fine French wine served at dinner…a revered and precious vintage of the highest quality.

The Ambassador, seated at his right, lifted his glass and drank the wine at one gulp.

King Edward gazed at him reproachfully, and admonished:

"Mr. Ambassador, when you meet a great wine of France you breathe it, hold it to the light, you touch it to your lips, you put your glass down and talk about it…."

As to talking about it, we have the story of the gourmet uncle who was entertaining his young sprig of a nephew, just home from college. Uncle, in his expansive hospitality, ordered a bottle of the finest wine in his cellar. Nephew partook of it without comment. Uncle began to think this precious nectar was wasted on the young squirt, so his next order to his butler was for an inferior wine.

Nephew seemingly drank this with relish.

"Fine wine, sir," he said. "Very excellent."

"Why, you young jackass," snorted Uncle. "The first bottle was beyond compare, but this stuff, bah!"

"I know," smiled the young man comfortably. "This one needs recommending, the other didn't."

## MORSELS

That all-softening overpowering knell,
The tocsin of the soul — the dinner bell.

*Lord Byron*

# DOUBLE, DOUBLE TOIL AND TROUBLE

*William Shakespeare, from Macbeth*

*One of the most famous recipes in literature, though not precisely*
*a gourmet's delight, certainly had the power to charm the partaker.*

  *First Witch.* Round about the cauldron go;
    In the poison'd entrails throw.
    Toad, that under cold stone
    Days and nights has thirty-one
    Swelter'd venom sleeping got,
    Boil thou first i' the charmed pot.
    *All.* Double, double toil and trouble;
    Fire burn, and cauldron bubble.
  *Second Witch.* Fillet of a fenny snake,
    In the cauldron boil and bake;
    Eye of newt and toe of frog,
    Wool of bat and tongue of dog,
    Adder's fork and blind-worm's sting,
    Lizard's leg and owlet's wing,
    For a charm of powerful trouble,
    Like a hell-broth boil and bubble.
    *All.* Double, double toil and trouble;
    Fire burn and cauldron bubble.
  *Third Witch.* Scale of dragon, tooth of wolf,
    Witches' mummy, maw and gulf
    Of the ravin'd salt-sea shark,
    Root of hemlock digg'd i' the dark,
    Liver of blaspheming Jew,
    Gall of goat, and slips of yew
    Silver'd in the moon's eclipse,
    Nose of Turk and Tartar's lips,
    Finger of birth-strangled babe
    Ditch-deliver'd by a drab,
    Make the gruel thick and slab:
    And thereto a tiger's chaudron,
    For the ingredients of our cauldron.
    *All.* Double, double toil and trouble;
    Fire burn and cauldron bubble.
  *Second Witch.* Cool it with a baboon's blood,
    Then the charm is firm and good.

# A TALE FROM THE PENNSYLVANIA DUTCH COUNTRY

*Ruth Hutchison*

Once a farmer's wife, who was very stingy, had a sly visitor who promised to tell her how to make delicious soup from a stone.

"First," he said, "find me a fine round stone." He washed the stone and dropped it in the kettle. "Now," he continued, "all we need are potatoes, cabbage and onions...some corn and string beans, too...some tomatoes, a little parsley, a dash of seasoning and, while you're at it, a good-sized piece of meat!"

Pennsylvania Dutch cooks still use their handwritten cook books. Except that nowadays they are usually written in English, they are very like the old ones. One is still likely to find a table of measurements in the front and a few household remedies in the back. The everyday recipes are skipped over without a qualm, but there is a spate of rules for cakes and pies, sweets and sours. The details of these are considered important, but, since anyone is supposed to be able to make the stews and pot roasts, they are gone over lightly.... This, of course, is why so many cherished Pennsylvania Dutch cook books appear to be a bit lopsided as to content. Gold cake, silver cake, sunshine cake, feather cake, sponge cake, angel food cake, devil's food cake, pound cake — so runs the list. Sweet dough, dumplings, noodles, soup balls — these you will find. But for a recipe for brown stew or pot roast you must search long and hard. Unless it is somehow unusual. For, certainly, there is no need to put down what everyone knows!

# THOMAS JEFFERSON ENTERTAINS

*Evan Jones*

In his five years in Paris, where he followed Benjamin Franklin as U.S. envoy, as much of Jefferson's attention as he could spare was devoted to recipes rather than treaties, to the intimate secrets of the kitchen rather than those of state. Jefferson, as Marshall Fishwick put it a little too neatly, "wed Virginian and French cooking in one of the happiest unions recorded in the history of cookery."

At any rate, he did his best to do so. It was Jefferson who ensconced the first French chef in the White House....

In his years as President, he took time when he could to oversee all phases of supply and preparation of White House food. "He would get out the wagon early in the morning," his overseer Edmund Bacon later wrote, "and [his steward] Lamar would go with him to Georgetown to market ...." Bacon emphasized that "it often took fifty dollars to pay the marketing they would use that day." At Monticello, according to Bacon, guests came "in gangs," with or without invitations, "and they almost ate him out of house and home....I have killed a fine beef and it would be all eaten in a day or two. There was no tavern in all that country that had so much company." Jefferson himself, said Bacon, "was never a great eater, but what he did eat he wanted to be very choice....He was especially fond of Guinea fowls, and for meat he preferred good beef, mutton, and lamb." With a sense of the history he played a part in, Bacon added that "Meriwether Lewis's mother made very nice hams. And every year I used to get a few from her for [the President's] special use."...

Margaret Bayard Smith, who played an active part in the first 40 years of the capital's social life, recalled long after Jefferson's death that the President's dinners were beyond comparison with any others given in the White House. She said succinctly that "Republican simplicity was united to Epicurean delicacy" in a style of hospitality not emulated often enough in the new nation. Seeing things differently, John Adams was nonetheless still impressed when he wrote: "I held levees once a week that all my time might not be wasted by idle visits. Jefferson's whole eight years was a levee. I dined a large company once or twice a week. Jefferson dined a dozen every day."

# NATURE'S GARDEN

*Nature provides a feast in the wild for those with the sense to discover it. Among the most well known advocates of a natural harvest is Euell Gibbons. Here he describes the delight of a good chew of seaweed.*

A weed-eater's experience is incomplete until he has learned to eat seaweeds. I've just returned from a week at the shore, and I am literally full of my subject and getting fuller all the time as I chew on a cud of dulse while I write. Dulse is a reddish seaweed known as *Rhodymenia palmata* to the botanist. I gathered my supply from a rocky tidepool in Maine and dried it in the sun. I chew it slowly, gently, and cautiously, so it won't disintegrate too quickly.

At first taste, dulse has a salty sea flavor, relished by many. But if chewed long and carefully, it gradually becomes permeated with a delightful sweet richness that greatly enhances one's enjoyment. A chemist friend tells me that this is due to the conversion of other carbohydrates into sugar by the diastase in the saliva. All I know is that the longer you chew on a bite of dulse, the better it tastes.

Dulse must be dried before it is edible. Fresh from the tidepool, it is tough and tasteless, giving the sensation of chewing on a salted rubber band. All that is necessary to tenderize and flavor it is a drying in the sun. On clear hot days I have dried dulse to edibility in six hours. One rainy day when I craved some, I put a little in an openwork onion bag and dried it an hour in the automatic clothes dryer. Dulse does not become brittle and crumbly when dried, but remains springy and flexible.

Most dulse is consumed by merely putting a wad of the dried fronds in the mouth and chewing on it tenderly, lovingly, and leisurely....

# A MAN FOR ALL SEASONS

*Ben Jonson*

A master cook! why, he is the man of men,
For a professor; he designs, he draws,
He paints, he carves, he builds, he fortifies,
Makes citadels of curious fowl and fish.
Some he dry-ditches, some motes round with broths,
Mounts marrow-bones, cuts fifty-angled custards,
Rears bulwark pies; and for his outer works
He raiseth ramparts of immortal crust,
And teacheth all the tactics at one dinner —
What ranks, what files, to put his dishes in,
The whole art military! Then he knows
The influence of the stars upon his meats,
And all their seasons, tempers, qualities;
And so to fit his relishes and sauces.
He has nature in a pot 'bove all the chemists
Or bare-breech'd brethren of the rosy cross.
He is an architect, an engineer,
A soldier, a physician, a philosopher,
A general mathematician.

# A RATIONLESS RENDEZVOUS

*Romilly Fedden*

A memorable dinner in France occurred during the war of 1914-1918. I was stationed at Boulogne at the time and there I met a charming old gentleman whose passion in life was fine china. He also owned a small factory for making china in an out-of-the-way part of Brittany. I happened to know the place, and this pleased him so much that nothing would do but that I come and dine with him. He explained that his house was now closed on account of air raids, but, if he could get hold of his cook, would I dine on Thursday next? If the cook could not be found he would wire me. No wire came, and next Thursday evening saw me at the gate of the old house in the *ville close*. I was ushered in by the aged housekeeper, our footsteps echoing loud down the empty passages. Through darkened rooms, past furniture swathed in dust-sheets, we reached at last a small room at the back of the house overlooking the garden. There my host, with the doctor and the abbé, awaited me.

We sat down to a wonderful meal. Our dinner started with a *bouillabaisse,* a mixture of *loup de mer,* red mullet, lobster and prawns — cooked in a casserole with white wine, saffron, garlic, onions, parsley, bay leaves and grilled crusts of bread. This was served as they do in Marseilles, *i.e.,* the broth and the fish residue were served separately. We drank, as I recall, a Meursault-Charmes. Then came partridges plainly roasted on toast, perfectly cooked, with red-currant jelly (the latter, I fancy, a sop to my English taste). At this point the old gentleman served a bottle of the famous Haut Brion of '75, insisting that we take a glass with our bird. There followed a crisp pale-yellow salad in a dark-blue bowl and a marvel of Camembert cheese; then fruit (such muscat grapes and peaches!) with which we drank a Château Yquem — surely the finest white wine in the world. Afterwards, coffee, and liqueurs on the terrace outside, facing a pale faintly green evening sky. Turning to me, the abbé smiled and slightly raised his glass, letting the brandy circle round behind his fingers. "We have," he said, "certain amenities in France, even in time of war." We sat back, not in silence, for even through the evening quiet of the garden stole the distant throbbing of the guns.

*Ben Jonson*

They drank pure nectar as the gods drink too,
Sublimed with rich *Canary*; say, shall then
These less than coffee's self, these coffee-men,
These sons of nothing, that can hardly make
Their broth for laughing, how the jest doth take,
Yet grin, and give for the vine's pure blood
A loathsome potion — not yet understood,
Syrup of soot, or essence of old shoes,
Dasht with diurnals or the book of news!

*Alexander Pope*

As long as Mocha's happy tree shall grow,
While berries crackle, or while mills shall go;
While smoking streams from silver spouts shall glide,
Or China's earth receive the sable tide,
While coffee shall to British nymphs be dear,
While fragrant steams the bended head shall cheer,
Or grateful bitters shall delight the taste,
So long her honors, name and praise shall last.

## MORSELS

Black as the devil, hot as hell,
pure as an angel, gentle as love.

Talleyrand

# THE WINE OF ISLAM

*William Harlan Hale*

Now the European table, enriched with great spice cargoes from the East and new foods from the Americas, was on its way to greater variety and flourish than had been known before. Another major innovation was to come in the seventeenth century — coffee.

The source of the coffee bean and the drink that was brewed from it appears to have been Ethiopia. From there it had spread through the Arab world, aided particularly by Mohammed's strictures against the consumption of wine: coffee was to be known as "the wine of Islam." Avicenna, famed eleventh century Arab physician and philosopher in remote Bokhara, was familiar with the drink (known to him as *k'hawah* and thought to have medicinal qualities).

# MORSELS

There is more simplicity in the man who eats caviare
on impulse than in the man
       who eats grapenuts on principle.

*G. K. Chesterton*


We may live without poetry, music and art;
We may live without conscience and live without heart;
We may live without friends; we may live without books;
But civilized man cannot live without cooks!

*Edward Robert Bulwer-Lytton*

# OLD WIVES' TALES

If a loaf of bread is found upside down,
there will be a death in the family.

Place a piece of wedding cake under your pillow;
you will dream of the man you will marry.

If it rains on a bride she will never stop eating.

Never borrow salt — especially on Friday.

Water in which eggs have been boiled or rinsed should not be used
for washing hands or face. It invites disaster.

Dishwater splashed on an apron
means one's future husband will be a drunkard.

Onions are said to induce dreams of a future husband or wife.

If one mince pie is eaten on each of the twelve days
of Christmas, twelve happy months will follow.

An apple a day keeps the doctor away.

You can expect a great fortune
if you discover a pod containing only a single pea.

Parsley has an unlucky reputation. It grows slowly and is said to go
nine times to the Devil. It grows best only for the wicked.

If your coffee forms bubbles while being poured, it means money
is coming your way. Sip the bubbles to insure the landfall.

# SHAPE UP OR SING AS A GROUP

*Dieting is an American pastime as popular as gourmet cooking. It requires, of course, a different frame of mind. No one knows just when "thin" became fashionable, or why. Here, humorist Erma Bombeck tries to explain how the overweight motivate themselves to achieve the illusive ideal of slenderness.*

The women in the Mortgage Manor housing development just started a Watch Your Weight group. We get together every Monday for coffee and doughnuts and sit around and watch each other grow. Somehow, it makes us all feel better to know there are other women in the world who cannot cross their legs in hot weather.

The other Monday after I had just confessed to eating half a pillowcase of Halloween candy (I still have a shoebox of chocolate bars in the freezer to go), we got to talking about motivation of diets.

"When my nightgown binds me, I'll go on a diet," said one.

"Not me," said another. "When someone compliments me on my A-line dress and it isn't A-line, I'll know."

"I have to be going someplace," said another woman. "I know as sure as I'm sitting here if someone invited me to the White House I could lose fifteen pounds just like that!" (Snapping her fingers)

"I am motivated by vacation," said another one. "I starve myself before a vacation so a bunch of strangers who have never seen me before can load me up with food so that when I return home I look exactly like I did before I started to diet."

"Home movies do it for me," said a woman, reaching for a doughnut.

"You mean when you see yourself and you look fat in them?"

"I mean when they drape me with a sheet and show them on my backside."

Finally, I spoke up. "There is only one thing that motivates me to lose weight. That is one word from my husband. My overeating is his fault. If he'd just show annoyance or disgust or say to me, 'Shape up or sing as a group,' I'd do something about it. I told him the other night. I said, 'It's a shame your wife is walking around with fifteen or twenty excess pounds. If things keep going on I won't be able to sit on a wicker chair. What are you going to do about it?' I asked, 'just sit there and offer me another cookie? Laugh at me. Shame me into it!

Humiliate me at parties!' Sure, I'd get sore, but I'd get over it and I'd be a far better, thinner person for it. Just one word from him and I'd be motivated!"

"Diet," he said quietly from behind his paper.

"Fortunately, that wasn't the word. Pass me another doughnut, Maxine."

I have dieted continuously for the last two decades and lost a total of 758 pounds. By all calculations, I should be hanging from a charm bracelet....

## LOVE AND COOKING

*Edward G. Danziger*

In later years I learned that love and cooking are the most important, the most basic, natural, and essential, as well as the most entertaining, pastimes in the world. Without love and cooking there would be no babies, no inheritance taxes, and no crepe suzettes. The course of affairs of the world has often been changed by a pretty woman and a good meal.

But don't think that because you can crack two eggs over a piece of bacon, you are a cook or that because you have a house full of children, you are a lover. Certainly not! because for love and cooking you must be born. There must be in your eyes, in your heart, and in your hands that special feeling, that special understanding and warmth, which can change night to day and rain to sunshine.

You may have learned to cook, you may possess a dozen cook books, and still you may not be a cook. You may have studied all the books on love and sex ever written...and still you may not be a lover, not be able to kindle the sublime fire that gives sense, soul, and fulfillment to our lives.

For love and cooking you must be born.

Set in Goudy Old Style, a typeface
designed by Frederic W. Goudy,
first issued by American Typefounders, 1914.
Printed on Crown Royale Book paper.
Designed by Myron McVay.